Rough Guides

25 Ultimate experiences

Places to Stay

Make the most of your time on Earth

ROUGH GUIDES

25 YEARS 1982–2007

NEW YORK • LONDON • DELHI

Contents

Introduction

EXPERIENCES have always been at the heart of the Rough Guide concept. A group of us began writing the books **25 years ago** (hence this celebratory mini series) and wanted to share the kind of travels we had been doing ourselves. It seems bizarre to recall that in the early 1980s, travel was very much a minority pursuit. Sure, there was a lot of tourism around, and that was reflected in the guidebooks in print, which traipsed around the established sights with scarcely a backward look at the local population and their life. We wanted to change all that: to put a country or a city's popular culture centre stage, to highlight the clubs where you could hear local music, drink with people you hadn't come on holiday with, watch the local football, join in with the festivals. And of course we wanted to push travel a bit further, inspire readers with the confidence and knowledge to break away from established routes, to find pleasure and excitement in remote islands, or desert routes, or mountain treks, or in street culture.

Twenty-five years on, that thinking seems pretty obvious: we all want to experience something real about a destination, and to seek out travel's **ultimate experiences**. Which is exactly where these **25 books** come in. They are not in any sense a new series of guidebooks. We're happy with the series that we already have in print. Instead, the **25s** are a collection of ideas, enthusiasms and inspirations: a selection of the very best things to see or do – and not just before you die, but now. Each selection is gold dust. That's the brief to our writers: there is no room here for the average, no space fillers. Pick any one of our selections and you will enrich your travelling life.

But first of all, take the time to browse. Grab a half dozen of these books and let the ideas percolate … and then begin making your plans.

Mark Ellingham
Founder & Series Editor, Rough Guides

25

Ultimate
experiences
Places
to Stay

Rustic luxury in the
BELIZEAN FOREST
01

THE STORY GOES THAT Francis Ford Coppola built Blancaneaux as a place to write, and it's hard to imagine a more inspiring base than this luxuriously rustic resort in Belize's Mountain Pine Ridge Forest Reserve. Just two or three hours' drive from the airport – or a short hop in your private plane – and you're poised for an idyllic few days where nature comes with all mod cons. Everything here seems designed to showcase the natural environment. Thatched cabanas scattered through the lush gardens, furnished with Central American textiles and artworks, feature decks and bathrooms half-open to the elements; thankfully, bedrooms are secured against mosquitoes and other nasties.

Twice a day, honeymooners and hikers alike troop up to the restaurant for tasty American breakfasts and Italian dinners, cooked using ingredients from the on-site organic garden. Staff will happily make you a packed lunch to enjoy while out exploring. Several of Belize's sights are within easy reach by 4WD, chief among them the ancient Maya city of Caracol – still under excavation – where you might find yourself wandering the overgrown ruins alone but for your driver-guide. Armed with every fact there is to know about Belizean history and wildlife, he'll regularly stop the car en route to point out a king vulture, perhaps, or to let you sniff the fragrant bark of a tree used in traditional medicines.

With so many activities to choose from, you'll need to set aside time to enjoy Blancaneaux for its own sake: lazing in a hammock overlooking the jungle, taking a dip in the natural pools formed by the Privassion Creek as it runs through the grounds, or hanging out in the bar, chatting with the guides about whether to go horse-riding, hiking or mountain-biking tomorrow.

However you spend your days, be sure to get up one morning while it's still dark. As the sky lightens and a misty scene comes into focus, parrots fly past, screeching an alarm over the sound of the rushing river. Sitting snuggled in a fleece on your deck, watching the jungle awaken before you in all its cawing, chirruping and whirring glory, is worth getting out of bed for.

need to know There are frequent flights to Belize City International Airport from US hubs such as Miami and Houston, from where you can take a bus to San Ignacio, the nearest town to **Blancaneaux**. For more information, check out ⓦwww.blancaneaux.com.

The Eagles may have sung about "standin' on the corner in Winslow, Arizona" – Standin' on the Corner Park supposedly marks the spot – but things at this desert outpost have been pretty sleepy since interstate I-40 supplanted Route 66.

Strange place, then, to find the most magical hotel in America. **La Posada** is the masterpiece of pioneering Southwestern architect Mary Jane Colter. For the last and greatest of the Fred Harvey company's railroad hotels, she was given the opportunity to create a showpiece property from the ground up, with complete control over everything from the overall design to the interior décor.

Although in reality the whole place was built in 1929, Colter gave it an intricate backstory, a romantic previous life as a Spanish-style hacienda laid out by a Hispanic cattle baron in the 1860s, expanded as he grew rich, and finally "converted" into a hotel. The sprawling complex combined Mexican antiques and local craftsmanship with the Art-Deco trimmings and fancy innovations expected by 1930s travellers. With the decline of the railroads, *La Posada* closed in 1957; Colter herself died a year later, after sadly observing "There's such a thing as living too long".

Forty years later, however, *La Posada* reopened, restored by enthusiasts who proclaim "we are not hoteliers – for us this is about art". This is no lifeless museum, however; it's bursting with earthy Southwestern style and imaginative adornments, not least the dazzling modernist canvases by co-owner Tina Mion that bedeck the public spaces. Each guest room is individually furnished – fittings range from hand-carved four-poster beds and inlaid wooden floors to deeply luxurious Jacuzzis – and named after illustrious former guests from John Wayne to Shirley Temple.

A fabulous restaurant, designed to mimic the dining car of the Santa Fe Railroad's Super Chief, and using Colter's original Pueblo-influenced tableware, serves contemporary Southwestern cuisine, using ingredients like Navajo-raised lamb and wild turkey. And irresistibly, this is still a railroad station, even if the former ticketing area and waiting rooms now serve as cosy public lounges; doors from the lobby lead straight to the platform, and the distant sound of train whistles provide a haunting backdrop to your slumbers.

need to know
Winslow, Arizona, stands sixty miles east of Flagstaff and a hundred miles west of Gallup, New Mexico. **La Posada** is at 303 E Second St (☎928/289-4366, ⓦwww.laposada.org); rooms start at $89 per night.

03 LAKESIDE ROMANCE IN
Rajasthan

India is teeming with wonderful places to stay, many of them tiny, old family-run homes transformed into romantic boltholes. It is rare, however, to find a large modern-day hotel with equal measures of soul, style and glamour. The arrival of Biki Oberoi's *vilas* properties in the state of Rajasthan has changed all that, creating a circle of confidence for nervous "but-won't-I-get-ill?" neophytes as well as a new kind of experience for old India hands.

These über-luxurious hotels are facing the future armed with spas, fancy food and twenty-first-century cocooning comforts. **Udaivilas**, situated in the achingly romantic city of Udaipur, is reached by canopied boat across shimmering Lake Pichola – arrive at dusk for the full effect. The grand Mewar-style building is a blaze of tinkling fountains, butter-coloured domes, reflective marble pools, pavilions and balconies. At night, flickering candles reflected in the water, the whole place evokes a bygone era of palaces and princes.

Despite all the must-do sightseeing it is hard to leave the hotel. Peacocks roam in the gardens, telepathic staff couldn't be cheerier, the shop is pashmina central, and rooms offer divine decadence.

The beds are vast, the marble baths deep, and local furniture and fabrics are beautifully crafted. You can even enjoy your very own mini infinity-edged pool, perfect for lazy lengths, with views of the City Palace, and a telescope to boot. If all this isn't enough, the hotel's Banyan Tree spa is a haven of ayurveda and aromatherapy. Every treatment begins with a foot scrub in rose-scented water, after which you can be wrapped in tomato or scrubbed with rice, enjoy marvellous massages or go yogic with the experts. As for the food – rejoice in fresh vegetables picked from the garden and fabulous meals ranging from fragrant curries to sophisticated Thai extravaganzas. Old hand or neophyte, you'll feast like there is no tomorrow – here is a hotel which satisfies everybody.

need to know

Prices start from $560 per room based on two people sharing. For reservations call ☎294 243 3300 or ⓦwww.oberoiudaivilas.com. You can reach Udaipur by plane via Delhi or Mumbai.

04
Sweet dreams Japanese-style

need to know
Kyoto is the best place to sample the ryokan experience. Book well in advance for **Hiiragiya** (⌨www.hiiragiya.co.jp) or **Yoshikawa Ryokan** (☎075/221-5544). Prices range from ¥30,000 to ¥60,000 ($260–500) per person

From the discreet entrance way to the tatami-mat guestroom, everything about a ryokan, a traditional Japanese inn, oozes understated elegance. You'll need a little knowledge of etiquette – and a few yen – to stay in one, but both are amply rewarded.

Sliding open the wooden front door, identified by a modest sign if at all, you enter a world of tinkling *shamisen* music and kimono-clad staff. Exquisite hanging scrolls and painted screens contrast with rustic woodwork and a seemingly casual arrangement of seasonal flowers soft-lit through shoji paper screens. It's an artful, quintessentially Japanese blend of refinement and simplicity.

Your shoes replaced with simple slippers, you'll be led along hushed corridors to your individually styled guestroom. It's stockinged feet only now on the rice-straw tatami mats. There's no sign of bedding, just a low table in an almost bare room. Attention is focused on the alcove, with its wall hanging and minimalist flower arrangement, and on the garden. For the full-blown ryokan experience, it's essential for the guestroom to look out on a traditional garden, no matter how small. Again it contains nothing flamboyant – no garish flowers, but a harmonious arrangement of moss, stone and neatly trimmed trees and bushes. If you are lucky, the forms and colours will be intensified by a recent rain shower: nature idealized.

The same attention to detail and sense of aesthetics is apparent in the food served. You'll be brought trays overflowing with meticulously balanced and presented seasonal delicacies. With its array of serving dishes and its delicate aromas a ryokan meal is as much a feast for the eyes and nose as for the taste buds. Don't just tuck in; savour the moment.

And the senses are in for one last treat before bedtime. The traditional Japanese bath is a ritual in itself. The basic rule is to scrub down thoroughly at the taps, then ease yourself into the cypress-wood tub full of piping hot water. Then simply soak. It's absolute bliss.

Returning to your room you'll find your futon has been laid out for you. Sleep comes in an instant, soothed by the gentle beat of the bamboo water-dripper nodding back and forth in the garden.

05
Serene decadence
in the heart of the Medina:
RIAD LIVING IN MARRAKESH

The route through Marrakesh's ancient walled city, the Medina, to the riad **Casa Lalla** takes you from the carnivalesque square, the Jemaa el Fna, through teeming back alleys where a bustling and exotic street life plays itself out before your eyes. As you walk by, children stop impromptu football matches to beg for coins, swathed women sitting cross-legged under umbrellas call to you, offering to tell your fortune, and butchers proffer pungent sheeps' heads. Don't be distracted by the little donkeys who struggle under startlingly heavy loads, or you'll forget to flatten yourself against the wall when the next dilapidated moped comes careering by. Immersed in this veritable street circus, your head will swim with everything that's strange and new: unfamiliar smells, a cacophony of exotic sounds, and even the light, which is brighter somehow. All thrilling – and exhausting.

Step inside *Casa Lalla* and suddenly you're a million miles away from the bazaar. This sumptuous, palatial home – riads are mansions arranged around a central courtyard garden, from which they get their name – is decorated with the rich fabrics, filigreed metalwork and carved cedar indigenous to the city. Olivier, the resident dog, makes himself comfortable in the main hall near the plunge pool and you'd do well to follow suit: lounge on the pillow-laden couches which cluster around the fireplace; take a glass of fragrant mint tea on the panoramic roof terrace; enjoy a massage in the traditional hammam. You may think you've reached the height of decadence, but the best is yet to come: at night, by candlelight, riad guests dine in these splendid surrounds on the haute French-Moroccan cuisine of the proprietor himself, who just happens to be a two-star Michelin chef. The food, presented in a six-course tasting menu, invented afresh every day, is, put simply, *magnifique*.

need to know

Casa Lalla, 16 Derb Jemaa, Medina, Marrakesh ☎061 08 37 13 ⊛www.casalalla.com. Doubles start around €100, but book ahead as there are only eight rooms. Dinner costs 400dh (about €30).

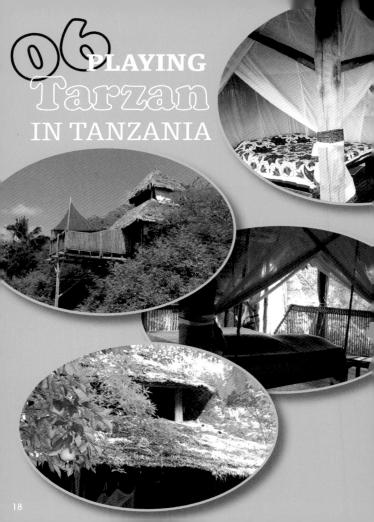

06 PLAYING
Tarzan
IN TANZANIA

Remember that incredible tree house you always dreamed of as a kid? The one hidden away in a jungle, set high up in the branches with a cool breeze rustling through the rooms and, in particularly inventive moments, surrounded by ancient ruins? The one that, despite your dad's best efforts with a hammer and a few pieces of plywood, never got any further than your imagination?

Well, that tree house exists. It might not be at the bottom of your garden, but it is on a paradise island marooned in the Indian Ocean, which comes a pretty close second. Tiny Chole Island, one of a cluster of reef-ringed islets that make up Tanzania's Mafia archipelago, is a place where you can swim alongside turtles and go to sleep at night thirty feet off the ground. Think Swiss Family Robinson with a little luxury. Hidden among a string of ruins – the crumbling, root-tangled legacy of a once-thriving trading centre – and set amid the upper boughs of immense baobab trees, these wooden wonders are the epitome of high-level living. The work of local dhow-builders, each one has a regal four-poster bed – some hanging from ropes, hammock style – on its top deck, just a few lazy steps from an elevated platform offering superb views over the mangroves and out into the sapphire sea beyond.

And after a hard day doing nothing, there can be few finer ways to end an evening than by gently swinging yourself to sleep, a dinner of fresh fish, octopus and lobster – cooked to perfection in rich Swahili sauces and served either up in your tree house or at lantern-lit tables dotted amongst the ruins – helping you on your way.

need to know

Chole Mijini (✆www.cholemijini.com) is reached by dhow from Mafia Island, which is itself a short flight from Dar es Salaam. A night in a tree house costs from $150 per person (including meals), a proportion of which goes to local community-run projects.

07

LIVE LIKE A DOGE:
one night at the Danieli

$\mathcal{V}$enice has more hotels per square kilometre than any other city in Europe, and for more than 150 years one particular hotel has maintained its status as the most charismatic of them all – the **Danieli**. Founded in 1822 by Giuseppe Dal Niel, it began as a simple guesthouse on one floor of the Palazzo Dandolo, but within twenty years it became so popular that Dal Niel was able to buy the whole building. Rechristened with an anagram of his own name, the hotel established itself as the Venetian address of choice for visiting luminaries: Balzac, Wagner, Dickens, John Ruskin and Proust all stayed here, and nowadays it's a favourite with the Film Festival crowd and the bigwigs of the art world who assemble for the Biennale.

So what makes the Danieli special?

Well, for a start there's the beauty of the Palazzo Dandolo. Built at the end of the fourteenth century for a family that produced four of the doges of Venice, the palazzo is a fine example of Venetian gothic architecture, and its entrance hall, with its amazing arched staircase, is the most spectacular hotel interior in the city. The rooms in this part of the *Danieli* are furnished with fine antiques, with the best of them looking out over the lagoon towards the magnificent church of San Giorgio Maggiore. This is the other crucial factor in the *Danieli*'s success – location. It stands in the very heart of Venice, right next to the Doge's Palace, on the waterfront promenade called the Riva degli Schiavoni, and in the evening you can eat at the rooftop *La Terrazza* restaurant, admiring a view that no other tables in town can equal.

All this comes at a price, of course: the *Danieli* is one of the most expensive places to stay in this most expensive of cities. There are three parts to the hotel: the old Palazzo Dandolo, known as the Casa Vecchia; an adjoining palazzo; and a block built in 1948. The best rooms, with lagoon views, are in the Casa Vecchia. If your Lottery ticket has come up, however, you might want to consider the delirious gilt and marble extravagance of the Doge's Suite – yours for around €4000 per night.

need to know

Hotel Danieli, Riva degli Schiavoni 4196, ☎041.522.6480.
Latest rates and reservations at ⓦwww.luxurycollection.com/danieli.

Chilling out
in the Icehotel
Sweden

08

The **Icehotel** is the only upmarket establishment in the world where you're guaranteed a frosty reception. Every October, huge chunks of crystal-clear ice are cut from Sweden's River Torne and pieced together, jigsaw style, at a spot along its northern bank. From December through to late spring, when the ice melts back into the river, the designer igloo opens its frozen doors to intrepid visitors, who travel deep inside the Swedish Arctic Circle for a night in this exceptionally cool hotel.

Pretty much everything in the entire complex, from the sculpted beds to the hotel's own chapel, is made out of ice; even the lights – intricately carved chandeliers – were once flowing water. While the overall effect is undoubtedly stunning, such sub-zero surroundings are hardly conducive to kicking back and relaxing awhile, so there are plenty of (expensive) activities to keep your circulation going.

By day, you can scoot off across the powder behind a pack of exuberant huskies, with only the sound of your sledge's runners gliding through the soft snow for company. By night, you can hop on your own snowmobile and head out into the inky blackness in search of the Northern Lights, their technicolour brushstrokes delivered with an artist's flick across the pristine sky.

Back at the hotel, there's just enough time to hit the Absolut Bar for a zingy Wolf's Paw cocktail, served in glasses carved – you guessed it – out of ice, before turning in for the night. With room temperatures hovering at a balmy -5°C, the interior designers have wisely gone for reindeer pelts and expedition-strength sleeping bags instead of crisp linen and home-brand hand lotions. You won't get a wink of sleep, of course, but then if it's a cosy night's kip you're after you've definitely come to the wrong place.

need to know

The **Icehotel** is in Jukkasjärvi, northern Sweden, 17km from Kiruna, the nearest domestic airport. Double rooms start at $300 (including breakfast). Most people spend one night here and one night in the nearby log cabins, which also start at $300. Check out ☻www.icehotel.com for details of excursions, and to book online.

09
Staying with a real-life
TRANSYLVANIAN COUNT

Driving to the remote Romanian village of Miklósvár, to stay in the guesthouse of Count Tibor Kálnoky, I started to feel like Jonathan Harker — the unsuspecting young lawyer in Bram Stoker's Dracula — who made a similar journey on such terrain to meet a different Transylvanian count. Even by car, rather than horse and carriage, the road has a nineteenth-century feel to it, being littered with potholes and random homebound livestock. Since my pleas for directions were answered with nothing more than indecipherable mumbles and sympathetic shrugs, I began to question the wisdom of my journey.

On my eventual arrival I was met, not by the count, but by his mysterious housekeeper (OK, actually a glamorous Scottish guide) and shown to my room, or rather house, all done up with beautifully restored Szekely antique furniture, and complete with a welcoming decanter of homemade plum brandy.

Heading into the candlelit wine cellar for dinner, I wondered whether, since it was now dark, we might clap eyes on the elusive count. But, after supping on delicious vegetarian goulash (carnivores had their own version), there was still no sign. Following a restful night under the downiest duvet imaginable, and a filling breakfast which included, of all things, muesli (a rare treat in Transylvania!), we finally got a glimpse of him, looking more as if he had stepped out of a Ralph Lauren catalogue than a Hammer movie and sporting a suntan that would seem to belie a fear of daylight. I fell immediately under his spell.

Speaking with an alluring aristocratic lilt – part Mitteleuropa, part transatlantic – and sounding nothing like Christopher Lee, the Count explained that while not immortal himself, his family has been in Miklósvár for centuries. Barred by the communists until 1989, he was later able to reclaim the family's former hunting lodge, previously a socialist "cultural" centre; he now uses the profits made from renting out the beautifully decorated guesthouses to restore it. When completed it will become an upmarket hotel in stunning grounds, with the family crest intact – rejuvenated here by tourists' interest and cash, rather than by their blood.

need to know
See ⓦwww.transylvaniancastle.com for details of tours and accommodation. Hungarian, rather than Romanian, is spoken locally.

Getting naked in Cap d'Agde

10

Awkward to pronounce, difficult to place on a map and virtually impossible to describe to friends when you return home, **Cap d'Agde**'s legendary nudist resort is one of the world's most unique places to stay. Of a size and scale befitting a small town, the Cap offers an ostentatious expression of alternative living. But this is no sect. The 60,000-odd naked people who come here during the height of summer often have nothing more in common than sunburnt bottoms and a desire to express themselves in unconventional ways.

The resort's sprawling campsite is generally the domain of what the French like to call *bios*: the hardy souls who arrive at the Cap when the nights are still chilly and leave when the last leaves have fallen from the trees. They love their body hair as much as they hate their clothes, are invariably the naked ones in the queue at the post office, and don't mind the odd strand of spaghetti getting tangled up in their short and curlies at lunch. These textile-loathing *bios* share the Cap with a very different breed, who are occasionally found at the campsite, but usually prefer the privacy of apartments or hotel rooms. During the day, these *libertins* gather at the northern end of the Cap's 2km-long beach. For them, being naked is a fashion statement as much as a philosophy: smooth bodies, strategically placed tattoos and intimate piercings are the order of the day – and sex on the beach is not necessarily a cocktail.

In the evenings, the *bios* prefer to play a game of pétanque, cook dinner and go to bed early. Meanwhile, as the last camp stoves are cooling down, a few couples might be spotted slipping out of the campsite dressed in leather, PVC, lacy lingerie and thigh-high stiletto boots to join the throngs of more adventurous *libertins* who congregate nightly in the Cap's bars, restaurants and notoriously wild swingers' clubs for a night of uninhibited fun and frolicking.

need to know

Cap d'Agde is on France's Mediterranean coast, 60km southwest of Montpellier. The *quartier naturiste* (nudist resort) lies on the northeastern edge of town. Accommodation is in self-catering apartments, hotel rooms or a large campsite.

11

GOING BUSH IN ONGAVA GAME RESERVE

Dinner in **Ongava Tented Camp** is always a memorable occasion: an open-air fireplace, a dozen or so guests, and, milling around the floodlit waterhole a few feet away, the evening's entertainment – an ageing bull elephant, maybe a rhino and her calf, or, on a lucky night, a pair of lionesses, returning from a hunt. Nestled at the foot of the tongue-twisting Ondundozonanandana Range, in Ongava Game Reserve, one of Namibia's largest private concessions, the intimate camp is everything you could ask for in an African safari experience: small and sumptuous – with just six tastefully furnished tents, each with an open-air bathroom for showering under the stars – and exhilaratingly wild.

The 75,000 acres of scrubby bush that surround the camp are prime territory for spotting both African species of rhino, as well as zebra, cheetah and a whole host of other smaller residents, including the rare black-faced impala. And once you've ticked those off your list, it's just a fifteen-minute drive to Etosha National Park, a salt pan the size of Switzerland, and one of Africa's truly great game parks, where you can add giraffe, kudu, leopard and ostrich to the roll call.

It's at night though, when the immense African sun has melted behind the hills and the sky is a thick, star-studded blanket of black, that *Ongava Tented* Camp really casts its spell. The campfire embers are slowly cooling and you're tucked up in a bed that wouldn't look out of place in a five-star hotel when the deep roar of a large male lion comes rumbling across the plains, washing over the canvas like a thunder clap. You're safe, of course, but the effect is still electrifying. That sound, that feeling, is one that you won't forget in a very long time.

need to know

Ongava Game Reserve is in the far north of Namibia. Staying at **Ongava Tented Camp** (ⓦwww.ongava.com) costs from $300 per person per night, including food and drinks and guided game drives. The best time for game viewing is in the dry season (July–Nov), when huge herds congregate around the parks' waterholes.

12 Wine and Horses of Estancia Colomé

Estancias are Argentina's proud answer to haciendas: working ranches with prize land stretching to the horizon, a stable full of thoroughbred horses and a distinctly noble flavour. Recently, a number of estancias have allowed guests to share their comforts while enjoying a back-to-nature experience. One such, the luxurious **Colomé**, is unusual in that it's also a winery. Not just any winery, but one of the world's highest, more than 2300m above sea level. The first grapevines, planted by the conquistadors in the sixteenth century, flourished thanks to the region's cool nights, warm, sunny days, and just the right amount of rain. Argentina's last remaining Spanish aristocrats ran the place in the nineteenth century. And then, as the world entered the new millennium, an ecologically minded Swiss entrepreneur turned *Colomé* into a luxury resort.

Nine modern suites form a neo-colonial quadrangle around a galleried patio and a gently gurgling fountain. Most afford sweeping views across to the snow-capped Andes, best enjoyed from a private veranda that looks directly onto a garden of native plants. *Colomé* manages to be spacious yet cosy – when the outdoor temperature drops, under-floor heating allows you to pad around barefoot. In any case, if you so wish, the butler will come with his bellows and light a fire in your very own hearth.

To discover the wild surroundings at a leisurely pace, tie on some chaps, mount a criollo steed and let Ernesto, a taciturn horse-whisperer from Chile, lead the way. Rides take you along dried-up riverbeds past thorny scrub with magnificent sierras as a backdrop. Flocks of parrots screech overhead. Gaudy butterflies sip at cactus blooms. Back at the ranch, you can meditate in the Zen room, take a dip in the turquoise pool, or admire the soothing works of avant-garde artist, James Turrell. And, most important of all, lose yourself in a ruby glass of 2004 Colomé malbec, while lounging in the gaucho bar. Then dinner is served…

need to know
Colomé (@www.estanciacolome.com) lies 25km from the secluded village of Molinos, in the far northwest corner of Argentina. The nearest airport, Salta (@www.turismoensalta.com), is 200km away, along a sinuous mountain road; some guests use the small airstrip or heliport nearby. The nightly rate is around $250 for a double; arrange accommodation and transport through Salta's leading travel operator, Marina Turismo (@www.marina-semisa.com.ar).

13 Locked up in Ljubljana: Hostel Celica

Fancy being banged up for the night?

Well, be Celica's guest. Born from the gutted remains of a former military prison, Ljubljana's Hostel Celica (meaning "cell") possesses a dozen or so conventional dorms, but it's the twenty two- and three-bed rooms, or more precisely, cells, that makes it so unique.

A range of designers was assigned to come up with themes for each one, resulting in a series of funky and brilliantly original sleeping spaces – one room features a circular bunk bed, for example, and in another a bunk is perched high above the door.

That's to say nothing of the wonderfully artistic flourishes, such as the colourful murals and smart wooden furnishings, that illuminate many of the rooms. Surprisingly, the cells are not at all claustrophobic, though some authentic touches, such as the thick window bars and metal, cage-like doors, remain – there's little chance of being robbed here.

The hostel stands at the heart of a complex of buildings originally commissioned by Vienna for the Austro-Hungarian army and which later served as the barracks of the former Yugoslav People's Army. Following Slovenia's declaration of independence in 1991, this complex was taken over by a number of student and cultural movements, evolving into a chaotic and cosmopolitan cluster of bars, clubs and NGOs collectively entitled Metelkova.

Despite repeated attempts by authorities to legalize, and even demolish, the site, the community has stood firm as the city's alternative cultural hub, with club nights, live music (punk, metal, dub/techno, lo-fi) and performance art all part of its fantastically diverse programme. Indeed, if you don't fancy the short stroll into Ljubljana's lovely old town centre for a few drinks, this makes a lively place to hang out before stumbling back to your cell. Just don't throw away the key.

need to know

Hostel Celica (☎01/430-1890; ⊛www.souhostel.com) is located on Metelkova ulica, just ten minutes' walk from the bus and train stations, and fifteen minutes' walk from the city centre. A bed in a cell costs €24 per night, a bed in a dorm room €17–21. Free tours of the cells take place daily at 1pm.

Getting Lost in the **14**
Pilgrim's Palace

Though you may well get lost in the sprawling **Parador de Santiago de Compostela**, you certainly won't mind if you do. This is medieval Spain in all its gold-flecked grandeur – a post-sherry saunter from the echoing banquet hall has you padding down crimson-carpeted hallways lined with heavy tapestries and presided over by stern-faced busts of a veritable who's who of Spanish history. And that's just one wing.

The golden-granite *parador* was built in 1499 for Queen Isabella and King Ferdinand as the Hostal dos Reis Católicos, a royal hospital that provided refuge and relief to all the foot-blistered pilgrims who streamed into this damp northwestern corner of Spain. Five centuries on, travellers still seek shelter here – though now high-thread-count sheets and heated towel racks are part of the package.

This hospice-turned-haute hotel is the grande dame of Spain's *paradores*, a chain of government-run hotels – now numbering nearly 100 – established in the 1920s. The aim was both to provide accommodation in Spain's more remote, pastoral areas, and to revive and maintain ancient edifices, from castles and convents to monasteries and manor houses, that might otherwise fall into ruin. Today, staying in a *parador* not only offers the chance to bed down in a historical monument, but also helps ensure its survival.

Suites here are fit for a king – literally: kick back on canopied, four-poster beds like those once warmed by Spanish monarchs, tug on a tassel to turn on the light, catch your reflection in an antique mirror. Having catered to devout pilgrims, the *parador* is awash in spiritual nooks: leafy, hushed cloisters offer moments of absolute stillness in the late afternoon, as shadows fall across the stone pillars, one by one.

The *parador* shares the Praza do Obradoiro with the city's splendid cathedral. All roads to Santiago lead to this Baroque behemoth, where the mortal remains of St James are supposedly buried. Roam the Romanesque interior – all the more memorable when the massive *botafumeiro* (incense burner) is being used: hung on ropes as thick as well-fed pythons, it's swung in a wide arc across the transept, a rite originally performed to perfume the disheveled, pungent pilgrims as they filed into the cathedral. These days, a scented bath at the *parador* should suffice.

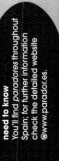

need to know
You'll find *paradores* throughout Spain, for further information check the detailed website ⊕www.parador.es.

15 MONASTIC
Mount Áthos

Leaving the boat I'd caught in Ouranoúpoli, the last Greek-Macedonian village before the border with the monastic republic of Áthos, I disembark at a small harbour. I toil uphill onto the peninsula's endangered cobbled-trail system, and find myself deep in broad-leafed forest – without mobile reception. An anxious hour ensues before a signal re-appears; it's essential to reserve a bed in advance at most of the mountain's twenty fortified monasteries.

Lunch, four hours later, is at Hilandharíou. The young monks at this thirteenth-century Serbian monastery are amazingly courteous considering that NATO has just flattened their country. Despite losing my way on overgrown paths, I reach ship-shape Stavronikíta on the north coast by nightfall, where I am offered a frugal meal of soup, salad, bread, and an apple – typical fast-day fare.

My room comes complete with snoring roommate; seeing my hesitation, the guest-master takes pity and lodges me in private quarters – until 3.30am, when a símandro (hammered-plank-bell) announces obligatory matins. After a 6am coffee and biscuit, I'm sent on my way – hospitality is for one

need to know
Only ten heterodox males are admitted to Mt Áthos each day, for a maximum of four days. Contact the Mount Athos Pilgrim's Bureau in Thessaloníki (☎2310 252578, ℻2310 222424).

night only – munching on the nuts and sesame cake Áthos trekkers use to keep their strength up.

Father Iakovos, the kindly, multilingual librarian at tenth-century Ivíron, greets me. I mention the disgraceful state of Athonite paths, and he offers me Philip Sherrard's monograph on their spiritual meaning. After lunch, a monastic jeep gives me a lift to Áthos's spectacularly rugged, roadless tip, where I stay at a primitive kellí (agricultural colony).

Next morning, in the echoing corridors of Ayíou Pávlou monastery, a small boy, brought along by his father, cries inconsolably for his mum – unluckily for him, the only woman allowed on the Holy Mountain is the Holy Virgin.

Dawn of my last overnight at Grigoríou, on the fourth day of July trekking, finds me filthy; Athonite guest quarters have no bathing facilities. (A particularly ripe medieval Orthodox monk, challenged about his hygiene, retorted, "I am washed once in the blood of Christ. Why wash again?").

Below the trail that takes me back to the boat, I find a secluded cove, strip naked, and plunge into the satiny Aegean. Miraculously, the Virgin does not strike me dead.

16 Soaking away
your troubles at the
Hotel Gellért

*Y*ou might be impressed by the stately location of the Hotel Gellért, just over the "Liberty Bridge" on the western bank of the Danube, anchoring the old section of Buda. You might enjoy this picturesque scene especially after dark (and you'll certainly feel compelled to take pictures) on your way back across the bridge from a night out in Pest: the entire, rambling building, frontlit, glows like some giant Art Nouveau birthday cake at the base of craggy Gellért-hegy cliff. You might be awed by the grand staircases leading from the lobby; charmed by the cozy, hideaway bar and its array of Hungarian liquors; spun around by the long corridors and various turns getting to and from your room (especially after a drink or two of Unicum at the aforementioned bar); satisfied by the size of the room – better still if it comes with a view of the river in front or hills behind. But none of this is by itself necessarily a reason to stay. There's a greater motivation for that.

Wake up early to find out, and pull on the robe that hangs in the closet. Go to the excruciatingly slow caged elevator on your floor. Tip the lift operator as you reach the bottom, exit and pick your way through the milling crowd to see what they're all waiting for. Don't be embarrassed about your state of relative undress – soon you'll all be in the same boat. Then – behold the glory of the Gellért baths.

The grandeur of the vaulted entry hall, its tiling, statuary and skylit ceiling, is a worthy precursor to the pools themselves. First, the segregated areas: a dip in the 34° waters, while admiring the magnificent mosaics and ornamental spouts; a sit down in the aromatic sauna; a bracing splash in a tiny, freezing cold bath, a plunge into another pool, this one 38° . . . Repeat the ritual again, then finish with some invigorating laps in the colonnaded central pool, the one place where the sexes intermingle. Consider doing the backstroke to best enjoy the light streaming through the retractable stained-glass roof above. And think about extending your stay another day or two.

need to know Hotel Gellért, Szent Gellért tér, District XI, Budapest (☏36 1 889-5500, ⊛www.danubiushotels.com/en/budapest-hotels/danubius-hotel-gellert-budapest). Double rooms start at €160; breakfast and access to the baths (6am–6pm) included. The baths themselves are operated independently of the hotel.

17

Kenya

Malewa River Lodge
Mountain-biking with the herds

How about a cool, low-key private game sanctuary, with delightfully eccentric lodgings built from mud, thatch, reclaimed timber and recycled ranch fencing? How about staying in your own cottage shaded by superb acacia trees, fronted by sloping lawns, close to a rushing river and not far from the Happy Valley of colonial days? **Malewa River Lodge**, set in Kenya's Kigio Conservancy, is such a place.

A recent, private venture that has converted a cattle ranch on the banks of the Malewa River into a thriving sanctuary for the kind of wildlife you can mingle with in relative safety, the Kigio Conservancy harbours a breeding herd of rare Rothschild's giraffe, good numbers of zebra, impala and waterbuck, and several charmingly inquisitive ostriches.

Staying at the lodge, you can rent mountain bikes, or take horses, and head off through the bush for a few hours, following an easy network of tracks and landmarks. In 2004 the BBC filmed the high-stakes translocation of a pair of white rhinos into Kigio, and you can track the docile couple, alone or with a guide. There are no large predators in the conservancy, which is fenced on three sides and bounded to the north by the river. Kids, and young-at-heart adults, are also wowed by the brown and churning Malewa itself.

The forest-swathed riverbank near the lodge harbours troupes of monkeys and dozens of species of birds, while a mini suspension bridge gives access to the foothills of the Aberdares, from where you can look out for the local pod of hippos. Head downstream and you come to a weir and waterfall and cliffs ideal for river-jumping.

The adventure doesn't end as night falls. Grab a torch to make your way through the bush. The *Malewa River Lodge* chef conjures excellent meals from fresh, local food, and they serve the best coffee in the Rift Valley. After dinner, you'll gather with the other guests to share animal stories by a huge fire. They have electricity at the office, but mostly your nights will be lit by the flicker of candles and kerosene lamps.

need to know

Between the gardens of Lake Naivasha and the flamingo spectacle at Lake Nakuru a modest sign on the highway points north to Kigio, where **Malewa River Lodge** (www.malewariverlodge.com) offers doubles from $210 for full board

18 Barefoot Bliss at Soneva Gili, Maldives

For being in, on, and with the sea, the wonderful water-world of the Maldives is hard to beat. A necklace of palm topped, sandy white islands in the Indian Ocean, from your sea-plane they look for all the world like Tiffany-blue floating poached eggs. Wonderfully secluded, these amazing atolls are home to some of the most luxurious, beautiful and expensive hotels in the world, each occupying its own small island.

Soneva Gili epitomizes the very best in barefoot luxury. If your idea of a hot hotel is marble bathrooms, golf courses and tables groaning under the weight of silver you've got the wrong place. We're talking Robinson Crusoe meets World of Interiors, a simple idyll finessed with lavish touches.

At *Gili* your shoes are gently removed upon arrival, the clocks are set an hour forward for maximum sunshine, and your food, spa, CD and pillow preferences are all established ahead via email. The wooden villas are castaway fantasies, spacious and deeply private, with walk-in wardrobes for all those clothes you'll never wear, breezy day rooms, and two bathrooms – one inside, one beneath the stars. Stay in a villa on stilts over the shimmering sea and you can row your own little canoe back to your room, sleep outdoors lulled by a balmy breeze, and order room service by speedboat – very James Bond.

Most pleasures here seem to be horizontal – sunbathing, swimming, snorkelling, scuba diving. You can also be dropped off at a deserted island for the day (hammocks and picnics provided), head off for a day of pampering at the spa, or simply chill in the pristine peace of your private pool.

The food is also sensational, much of it grown in the resort's own vegetable garden, with bread straight from the oven, sushi and oysters, zingy fresh fish, and French wines. Feast in the candlelit privacy of your veranda or on a remote starlit sand-spit that's here today, gone tomorrow.

need to know The island appears to be miles from anywhere. In reality it's fifteen minutes by speedboat from Male airport, which is served by direct flights from London. Prices start from $1000 per night for a Villa Suite including service, a bottle of champagne and a twenty-minute spa treatment.

A night with the Iban

19

Staying in a Longhouse

Borneo

Sleeping in a longhouse can be uncomfortable. You'll find yourself bedding down on a scratchy mat on a wooden floor, with the odd nail nudging your spine for good measure. It helps if you're the sociable type – the rest of your tour group will probably be right next to you. So what's the appeal? Far more than just a place to sleep, the longhouse offers an insight into Malaysian tribal society, which, although well hooked into modern ways – you will find DVDs and TVs in most longhouses – still cherishes its traditions.

In the east Malaysian state of Sarawak many of the indigenous population live in these longhouses, situated on rivers set deep within the dense, forested interior. The buildings are elegant, but home-spun; sturdy enough to sustain the fiercest monsoon downpours. Getting to them is a thrill in itself, involving a trip by motorized longboat complete with a scout whose job it is to look out for sharp rocks. Once there, visitors are met by the chief (*tuai*) and taken onto the communal veranda. Everyone gets a welcome drink, usually a glass of rice wine (*tuak*), or if it is a Christian community, orange squash. Mats make do for seating as well as bedding.

Meals, taken with the chief's family, usually consist of rice, meat, local jungle ferns and tropical fruits, like papaya, mango and rambutan. If you're lucky, a hunting party might have returned with a wild boar, which will be roasted, on a spit. As a guest, you'll be offered the best, fattiest chunks.

During the day, tours head out to local orchards, or you can sit with the Iban women as they spin rattan baskets and fabrics on the longhouse veranda. After a day with your hosts, full to bursting with food and drink, you won't care much about the scratchy mat and the nails. You'll awake to the sounds of tropical birds and the jungle emerging from the morning mist: mysterious, deep green and wildly scented. You'll feel like you've discovered a lost world.

need to know

Years ago, travellers turned up at longhouses and slept on the veranda for free. Nowadays, however, everyone visits in a tour group. Numerous companies are based in Sarawak's main cities. **Borneo Adventure** (Ⓦwww.borneoadventure.com) and **Diethelm Travel** (Ⓦwww.diethelmtravel.com) are both in Kuching. Reckon on around $150 per person per night for travel, board, activities and food.

The 20 BURJ AL ARAB
shows off in DUBAI

Dubai is a desert turned Disney.

What was once a sleepy fishing village is now a futuristic cyber city, with sparkling skyscrapers, shopping malls, water parks, golf courses, and hotels so flashy that Elton John would be proud to call them home. Top of the lot is the iconic **Burj Al Arab**, a striking 28-storey symbol of new-world bling. The gleaming building, the tallest hotel in the world, is shaped like a billowing sail – and to say it dominates the skyline is an understatement. At night, surrounded by choreographed fountains of water and fire, it is truly spectacular.

Start as you mean to go on with a Rolls Royce pick-up from the airport and you will swiftly get the picture. Huge tropical aquariums and backlit waterfalls dominate the lobby, the carpets are a whirl of lurid reds, greens and blues, and on-site stores glitter with diamonds and emeralds. Modestly marketed as "the world's first seven-star hotel", it has a helipad on the roof (where Federer and Agassi played out that tennis match) and more than 1200 staff poised to satisfy your every whim.

need to know

Rates depend upon which category of suite you book. For further information see ®www.burj-al-arab.com.

The bedrooms are all gigantic suites, their decor the epitome of Arabian kitsch. We're talking mirrors above the beds, leopard-print chairs and gold-tapped Jacuzzis in every bathroom. The 42-inch TV screens are framed in gold and the curtains and doors can be operated electronically. If all this doesn't quite cut it for you, the two show-stopping Royal Suites come with their own private elevators, cinemas and rotating beds. A bargain at $28,000 per night.

When it comes to food, naturally your personal butler can rustle up anything you desire, or you might prefer to take a three minute-trip in a simulated submarine to the underwater restaurant. Oh, and don't miss a drink in *Burj Al Arab*'s famous bar, situated on the 27th floor, 200m above sea level. From here you can gaze across at The Palm and The World – extraordinary manmade islands shaped like their namesakes and prime real estate to some of the wealthiest people on the planet.

The *Burj Al Arab* is the ultimate in ostentatious opulence. Embrace the excess and smile.

21

Star-gazing at the
Termas de Puyuhuapi

It can take you days to reach the Termas de Puyuhuapi – but then getting there is all part of the fun. One of the remotest hideaways in the world, the luxurious lodge-cum-spa sits halfway down Chile's Carretera Austral, or "Southern Highway", a thousand-kilometre, mostly unpaved road that threads its way through a pristine wilderness of soaring mountains, Ice Age glaciers, turquoise fjords and lush temperate rainforest. The most exciting way to travel down it is to rent a 4WD – you'll rarely get above 30km per hour, but with scenery like this, who cares?

Separated from the Carretera by a shimmering, pale-blue fjord, the lodge is unreachable by land. Instead, a little motor launch will whisk you across in ten minutes. It's hard to imagine a more romantic way to arrive, especially during one of the frequent downpours that plague the region, when guests are met off the boat by dapper young porters carrying enormous white umbrellas.

The hotel is made up of a series of beautifully designed low-lying buildings constructed in local timber with lots of glass, blending in handsomely with their surroundings. Having come quite so far to get here it would be a shame not to splash out on one of the eight shoreside rooms, with their mesmerizing views across the fjord. Inside, it's all understated luxury: flickering log fires, bare wooden floors, sofas to sink into, light streaming in from all directions.

You can take to the wilderness in a number of ways: go sea-kayaking (with dolphins, if you're lucky); learn to fly-fish in secret rivers packed with trout and salmon; take a hike through the rainforest to a nearby glacier. And afterwards soak your bones in the hotel's *raison d'être*, its steaming hot springs, channelled into three fabulous outdoor pools – two of them right on the edge of the fjord, the other (the hottest of all) enclosed by overhanging ferns. Lying here at night, gazing at the millions of stars above, you'd think you were in heaven. And really, you'd be right.

need to know

Rooms at the Termas de Puyuhuapi (☎67 325103, ⊛www.patagonia-connection.com) start at $134 a night. If you don't want to drive there, the hotel offers packages including transfers from the tiny airport of Balmaceda, 280km (5hr) south of Puyuhuapi.

A taste of rum in
Kinloch Castle

Scotland isn't a country that's short of fairy-tale castles, and you don't have to be a prince or a prisoner to get to stay in one. Some have been transformed into smart hotels or holiday lets, but it's worth remembering that romantic medieval digs are rather more compromised by draughts, awkward layouts and endless staircases than your average Holiday

Top of the pile of weird and wonderful piles must come Kinloch Castle on Rum. Rum is a spectacular but sparsely populated island just south of Skye. Named not by pirates but the Vikings, who described it as "wide", its empty glens and distinctive peaks once formed a noted sporting estate. In the late nineteenth century one particularly extravagant owner, Sir George Bullough, set about building a grand castle to house himself and his wealthy chums whenever they fancied bagging a few stags and living it up with their mistresses and racing cars. Built in red sandstone with crenellations, turrets and all kinds of early mod-cons including double glazing, central heating and electricity, *Kinloch Castle* was as extravagant as it was out of place. Not many of the rugged Hebridean islands can boast a billiard room, a barrel organ and palm houses.

Between the wars the spendthrift aristos retreated to places less wild and remote, and both Rum and *Kinloch Castle* are now in the hands of the conservation body Scottish Natural Heritage. The castle is a bit of a millstone, in truth, a unique piece of architecture but now falling to bits. The interiors remain largely intact with their threadbare Edwardian furnishings, and the servants' quarters are used as a hostel for visitors and volunteer conservation workers. A few larger rooms act as communal lounges and by special arrangement it's still possible to stay in grander style in some of the original guest bedrooms. You'll feel sympathetic to the castle's plight more than overwhelmed by its opulence, bewildered by its eccentricity rather than enchanted. But there is, after all, a shadow side to all fairy tales.

need to know

Ferries to Rum run daily from Mallaig and, in summer, from Arisaig. There are usually guided tours of Kinloch Castle every afternoon. Accommodation in the castle is akin to an independent hostel, with beds from £13 per night and meals available. Phone ☎01687/462037 or see ⓦwww.hostel-scotland.co.uk.

23 Vacation Like a Drug Lord in Tulum, Mexico

Even drug kingpins – perhaps especially drug kingpins – need a little time away from it all. The late Pablo Escobar, the Colombian drug lord once ranked as the seventh richest man in the world by Forbes, favoured beach getaways. In the 1980s, he built an airy, eight-bedroom mansion just footsteps away from the ocean in the one-street town of Tulum, about 100km south of Cancún on Mexico's Caribbean coast.

need to know

Nightly rates range from $185 to $235, but vary (greatly) by season. Ask also about weekly rates. The entire house may be rented for a (very negotiable) $26,000 per week, all-inclusive. You can see rooms at @www.amansala.com/version-2/accommodations-casa.html. Contact the owners at ✉casamagna@amansala.com or ☎011 52 9841 000 805.

In 1993, after Colombian police killed Escobar in a shootout in Medellín, his Tulum mansion, nicknamed **Casa Magna**, became the property of the Mexican government. Over the next decade, as the town around it evolved into an eco-friendly, yoga-centric beach paradise, *Casa Magna* fell into disrepair. Finally, in 2005, Mexico leased the house to the owners of Amansala, a Tulum resort best-known for its yoga-and-fruit-shake bikini bootcamps. Amansala's owners – Americans Melissa Perlman and Erica Gragg – painstakingly renovated the villa, replacing its rustic drug-dealer style with minimalist Asian beach-chic.

Ironically, the former kingpin's party house has become perhaps the quietest, most understated resort in what's now known as the "Mayan Riviera". This is the place to sit back and enjoy the white sand, gentle waves and warm water of the Caribbean – and a wide array of the most comfortable beach furniture on earth.

Take care when choosing a bedroom, however, as *Casa Magna*'s rooms are numbered, essentially in order of desirability, from one to eight. The secluded room one must have been Pablo's – its two private decks offer views of both the ocean and the sunset. The dark, viewless room eight, on the other hand, was surely the domain of tag-alongs and lowly members of his extended posse. If the room available is numbered higher than six, you may want to seek alternative accommodation – luckily, the equally stunning **Casa Magna Two**, Pablo's second vacation home, is just down the road.

Bed, barracuda and breakfast:

Jules' Undersea Lodge

Jules' Undersea Lodge – named after the intrepid aqua-explorer Jules Verne – began life as a research lab off the coast of Puerto Rico in the 1970s; it was moved to the Florida Keys and converted to its current use in 1986 by a pair of diving buffs and budding hoteliers.

A pod that sits a few feet above the lagoon floor, the lodge has just two smallish guest bedrooms, fitted out with TVs, VCRs and phones and hot showers, plus a fully equipped kitchen and common room. All very ordinary – except, of course, that you are 21 feet below the sea. Expert scuba divers can spend up to 22 hours exploring the marine habitat each day – safety regulations permit no longer than that; first-timers, meanwhile, need only need take a three-hour tutorial on the basics of underwater swimming and survival before they can duck down for check-in.

(Fitful types will sleep with the fishes far more restfully knowing that there's 24-hour safety monitoring from land nearby.)

Guests (or "aquanauts" as the lodge-owners call them) must swim down to reach the lodge, which, shaped like a figure of eight, has a small opening on the base in the center. Your first point of arrival is into a wet room; the disconcerting sensation is much like surfacing from a swimming pool, except, of course, that you're still underwater. Compressed air keeps the sea from flooding in.

Once ensconced in this enclave, most guests spend their time gazing out of the enormous, 42" windows in the lodge's hull: these vast portholes make a spectacular spot to spy on its surroundings. *Jules' Lodge* is anchored in the heart of a mangrove habitat, the ideal nursery for scores of marine animals, including angelfish, parrotfish and snapper; meanwhile, anemones and sponges stud the sea floor. Anyone too busy fish-spotting to whip up a spot of dinner needn't worry, as there's a chef on hand who can scuba down to prepare meals; or, for late night munchies, a local take-out joint offers a unique delivery service – perfectly crisp, underwater pizza.

need to know

Jules' Undersea Lodge, Key Largo Undersea Park, 51 Shoreland Drive, MM-103.2, Key Largo, Florida ☎**305/451-2353,** ⊛**www.jul.com. Overnight stays cost $445 per person; lunch only $165 per person.**

The Secret Sensation of Pousada Maravilha, Brazil

Fernando de Noronha is an impossibly beautiful secret island just an hour's flight from Recife in northern Brazil. A pristine National Marine Park, it was once visited by Charles Darwin and is so eco-orientated that on some beaches no sun cream or flip-flops are allowed. It has long been a hideaway for the Brazilian jetset, and is all the more alluring because the number of visitors permitted entry is limited to just 400 a day. Mention the island to any Brazilian and they will sigh with longing. UNESCO has measured the air as the second-purest in the world after the Arctic.

Until recently, the island's only weakness was the lack of a decent hotel. Thus the **Pousada Maravilha**, owned by the scions of some of Brazil's wealthiest families, is reason to rejoice. There are just eight white, bright rooms, very contemporary, and all with billowy curtains and bouncy beds. Views stretch out onto a brilliant peacock-green ocean, and you can enjoy outdoor jungle showers, a private Japanese hot tub and lazy-time hammocks. If you can bear to leave your room, the sleek infinity-edged pool is rock-star cool, with funky low level day beds and more of those awesome views.

During the day your best bet is to hire a beach buggy, bomb around on roads blissfully free of traffic lights, and discover the most breathtaking deserted beaches – many of them lurking at the end of bumpy dusty tracks, and some with cavorting dolphins. Divers will delight in the gin-clear water – visibility up to 50m – and ridiculously rich marine life; those who prefer to stay on shore can

watch Green Sea baby turtles hatch on the beach in the dead of night. Showtime runs from December to May.

Returning to your hotel is the ultimate treat. Candlelit massages are knock-out; suppers waist-expanding. The staff are so accommodating that they even check you in for your flight out, so you only have to face the airport minutes before departure. Heaven.

need to know
There are daily flights to the island from both Recife and Natal; the hotel (☎+55 81 3619 0028; @www.pousadamaravilha .com.br) is then five minutes' drive from the airport. Rooms cost from around $400 a night, including breakfast and

Ultimate
experiences
Places
to Stay
miscellany

1 From one extreme to another

Perched among the peaks of the Himalayas, at a dizzying 3960m above sea level, Hotel Everest View is the **highest hotel on the planet**. At the other end of the spectrum, Jordan's Mövenpick Resort and Spa, arguably the most stylish hotel on the Dead Sea, lies at the **lowest place on the planet**, some 400m below sea level.

Circuit House is one of only two hotels in Cherrapunji, India, which, with a record-breaking 26.5m of rainfall in one year, is the **wettest place on earth**. An altogether more arid option is the Explora Atacama; the luxury hotel lies at the heart of Chile's Atacama Desert, the **driest desert on earth**.

The **biggest hotel in the world** is First World Hotel in the Genting Highlands, Malaysia. It has a total of 6118 rooms and boasts 46, 450 square metres of indoor theme park, shopping centres, casinos and restaurants. If you're looking to downsize a little, the Grand Hotel de Kromme Raake in Eenrum, The Netherlands, is the **smallest hotel in the world**, with just one room.

Hoshi Ryokan, a traditional Japanese establishment in the heart of Ishikawa Prefecture, Japan, is the **world's oldest hotel**; it has been receiving guests since AD 717.

2 Instant karma

▶▶ Five lodgings for inner peace

- **Valvanera monastery** in La Rioja, Spain
- **Xixiang Chi Taoist temple** on Emei Shan, China
- **Ketura kibbutz** in the Arava Valley, Israel
- **Basilica di Superga** church in Turin, Italy
- **Haiensa Buddhist temple** in Hapcheon-gu, Korea

3 **Shaken not stirred**

Several hotels are famous for their own cocktails, but arguably the best-known of them all is the Singapore Sling, created by Ngiam Tong Boon at the Raffles Hotel in Singapore in 1910. Such is its notoriety that, nowadays, the cocktail is premixed by the dozen; sipping on a "sling" in the Raffles' Long Bar will set you back around $12.50.

▶▶ **Famous hotel cocktails**

Singapore Sling Raffles Hotel, Singapore

3 oz pineapple juice
1 oz gin
½ oz cherry brandy
¼ oz Benedictine
¼ oz Cointreau
¼ oz lime juice
1 dash Angostura bitters

$10,000 Martini Algonquin Hotel, New York City

5 parts gin
1 part dry vermouth
1 diamond from the in-house jeweller, Bader & Garrin

Ramos Gin Fizz Roosevelt Hotel (now the Fairmont), New Orleans

2 oz gin
2 oz cream
1/2 oz lemon juice
1 egg white
2 tbsp powdered sugar
3 dashes orange flower water

White Lady Savoy Hotel, London

½ dry gin
¼ Cointreau
¼ lemon juice

▶▶ The world's most expensive mini bars

A can of Coca-Cola will cost around:
- €10 at the Ritz, Paris
- €8.15 at Byblos, St Tropez
- €6.70 at Claridge's, London
- €6.10 at George V, Paris
- €5.95 at the Metropolitan, London

4 A spooky stay

The Schooner Hotel in Alnmouth has twice been named the **Most Haunted Hotel in Britain** by The Poltergeist Society. The 400-year-old hotel has 32 rooms – and an estimated 60 ghostly guests. Paranormal reports include lights and doors operating on their own, the appearance of orbs, cold spots, and phantom apparitions. Rooms 16, 28 and 30 allegedly receive the most activity.

5 Iconic views

Ngorongoro Crater Perched on the very rim of Tanzania's incredible crater, Ngorongoro Crater Lodge affords sublime views down into the caldera – and that's just from the loos.

Macchu Pichu Sanctuary Lodge is the only hotel within the confines of Peru's most famous Inca citadel.

The Great Wall of China Great name, even greater views: the Kommune by the Wall Kempinski looks out across a private section of unreconstructed wall, 30km north of Beijing.

The Pyramids of Giza The Mena House Oberoi sits in the shadows of these ancient Egyptian wonders.

Uluru All the luxury tents at Longitude 131° enjoy uninterrupted views of Uluru across the Australian Outback.

6 Camping

▶▶ Top tent tips

- For new tents, internal frames should be reduced by one or two percent to allow for canvas shrinkage.
- Avoid pitching your tent under trees, as some tree resins can damage canvas.
- A tent with mildew will leak. If your tent gets mildew on it, mix 480ml of bleach with 7.5 gallons of water and apply to the affected area.

▶▶ Five great places to pitch a tent

- St Martins, Isles of Scilly, Cornwall
- Angel Island, California
- Parque Nacional Torres del Paine, Chile
- Fraser Island, Australia
- Your back garden

7 Big screen and small print

▶▶ Just like the film

Star Wars The interior of Luke Skywalker's home, on the desert planet of Tatooine, is actually one of the inner courtyards of the Hotel Sidi Driss, in Matmata, Tunisia.

Pretty Woman The fire escape that Richard Gere climbs at the end of the film is attached to the Las Palmas Hotel in Los Angeles, USA.

Lord of the Rings The woods of Lothlorien, where Frodo seeks help from Galadriel, are the gardens of Fernside Lodge, near Wellington, New Zealand.

Octopussy The island home of Octopussy is the Taj Lake Palace on Lake Pichola, India.

Mission: Impossible Max's headquarters are based in the Hotel Europa, in Prague, the Czech Republic.

▸▸ Inspirational stays

Most people take a good book with them when they stay in a hotel; some end up writing one. Charles Dickens wrote **The Pickwick Papers** at The Angel Hotel in Bury St Edmunds; Charles Darwin began **The Origin of Species** while staying at the Kings Head Hotel on the Isle of Wight; William Burroughs wrote **The Naked Lunch** at the El Muniria Hotel in Tangiers; Arthur C. Clarke penned **2001: A Space Odyssey** in the Chelsea Hotel in New York; and Stephen King wrote **The Shining** in the Stanley Hotel in Colorado.

"The great advantage of a hotel is that it's a refuge from home life."

George Bernard Shaw

8 Alternative hotel transfers

- **Husky sled** from Kiruna Airport, Sweden
- **Cyclo rickshaw** from Da Nang airport, Vietnam
- **Seaplane** from Malé International airport, the Maldives
- **Fire engine** from Edinburgh and Glasgow airports, Scotland
- **Rubber dinghy** from Baltra aiport, the Galapagos Islands

9 Youth hostels

The **first youth hostel** was opened in Germany in 1909 by Richard Schirrman, a German schoolteacher.

The Youth Hostels Association of Great Britain was formed as a joint initiative between rambling, cycling and youth organizations; it is now known as the **YHA** (🅦www.yha.org.uk) and serves England and Wales, with separate associations for Scotland and Ireland. There are 227 youth hostels and 53 camping barns in England and Wales; between them they receive visitors from more than 80 countries each year, accounting for 500,000 overnight stays.

The YHA is part of **Hostelling International** (HI), the largest budget accommodation network in the world. It covers 60 countries, boasts 3.2 million members worldwide and even runs its own international campaign – Youth Hostelling for Peace and International Understanding. Volunteers are required to complete three-month missions as Ambassadors of Peace at one or more of the eleven HI Learning Centres for Peace, which – justifiably enough – include the youth hostels in Enniskillen (Northern Ireland), Verdun (France), Dachau (Germany) and Hiroshima (Japan).

10 **Wacky weekenders**

▶▶ **Five alternative accommodations**

In a prison Hotel Langholmen in Stockholm, Sweden, was once a penitentiary; clocks in reception display the time in Alcatraz, Sing Sing, Robben Island and Port Arthur.

Underwater Sleep with the fishes at The Utter Inn, ten feet below the surface of Lake Mälaren in Västerås, Sweden.

In a lighthouse Rose Island Lighthouse, a mile off the Rhode Island coast in the USA, lets you be a "volunteer keeper" if you stay for a week or more.

In a crane You choose the view at the Havenkraan van Harlingen, a crane that towers 17m above Harlingen harbour in The Netherlands: manoeuvring a control stick in the crane's cabin rotates the "hotel" through 360 degrees.

On the move Hop aboard the Exploranter, a mobile hotel truck with 28 beds, as it tours Patagonia and the Pantanal.

11 **"How much does a room cost?"**

Spanish ¿Cuanto es un habitación?

Hindi Kamraa kaa bhaaraa kyaa hai?

Vietnamese Cái này bao mốt phòng nhiêu?

Hungarian Mennyibe egy szoba kerül?

Swahili Pesa chumba ngapi?

12 Size counts and money matters

Eight out of the ten largest hotels in the world are in Las Vegas. The largest is First World Hotel in the Genting Highlands, Malaysia (see item 1 in this Miscellany), followed by MGM Grand Hotel Casino in Vegas, with 5690 rooms, and Ambassador City Jontiem in Pattaya, Thailand, with 4631 rooms. The other seven – all in Las Vegas – are Luxor Hotel Casino (4408 rooms), Mandalay Bay (4341), The Venetian (4027), Excalibur (4008), Bellagio (3993), Circus Circus (3774) and Flamingo Las Vegas (3565).

▶▶ Forbes' five most expensive hotel suites

Suite per night	What you get	How much it costs
Penthouse Suite Hotel Martinez, Cannes, France	▶▶ Four bedrooms, a private Jacuzzi and a huge terrace with views of the Mediterranean	$37,200
Royal Penthouse Suite President Wilson Hotel, Geneva, Switzerland	▶▶ A private elevator, bulletproof doors and windows and panoramic views over Lake Geneva	$35,000
Royal Villa Grand Resort Lagonissi, Athens, Greece	▶▶ Three bedrooms, two pools and a private gym	$34,088
Presidential Suite Hotel Cala di Volpe, Costa Esmeralda, Italy	▶▶ Three bedrooms, an outdoor saltwater pool and a private gazebo and solarium	$27,277
Bridge Suite Atlatris, Paradise Island, The Bahamas	▶▶ Ten rooms, including his 'n' hers bathrooms	$25,000

13 Five ethical abodes

Toilogt Ger Camp

Stay in a traditional *ger* (Mongolian tent) on the shores of Hovsgol Lake, the deepest lake in Central Asia. First tourist camp in Mongolia to run on solar energy; owned, managed and run by Mongolians.

Chumbe Island

Seven palm-thatched luxury lodges overlooking east Africa's best-preserved coral reef. Solar power; composting toilets; provides educational trips for local school children.

Elsewhere

Luxury beach accommodation in a wild setting in southern Goa. Low impact; local ownership keeps land free from large-scale development.

Chalalán Ecolodge

Spot caiman, monkeys and macaws deep in the Bolivian Amazon. Managed by the indigenous Quechua-Tacana community; share of the profits goes to the local village.

Damaraland Camp

Venture out from your luxury tent to track desert-adapted elephants. Run by the Damara community; ensures the survival of the Torra Conservancy in Namibia.

14 Seven stars

Designed to resemble a billowing sail, the Burj al Arab, in Dubai, was the first seven-star hotel in the world. Facilities for each two-storey suite include a personal butler, a chauffeur-driven Rolls Royce, and a "pillow menu" featuring a choice of thirteen pillows and quilts. For more, see p.46.

"When I am ill- natured, I so enjoy the freedom of a hotel where I can ring up a domestic, give him a quarter and then break furniture over him."

Mark Twain

15 To sleep, perchance to dream

▶▶ Five sleep-related facts

- A complete sleep cycle (one cycle contains five stages, each representing different brain patterns) lasts around ninety minutes. During an average sleep period, a person will experience four to five complete sleep cycles.

- In 1964, Randy Gardner, a 17-year-old American high-school student, stayed awake for a record-breaking 264 hours. Four days into his attempt, he began hallucinating and thought he was a famous American footballer.

- The snore of Melvin Switzer, an ex-British Snoring Champion, measures 92 decibels – louder than a pneumatic drill.

- Ten percent of snorers have sleep apnoea, a sometimes life-threatening disorder that causes sufferers to stop breathing up to 300 times a night.

- Before Thomas Edison invented the light bulb in 1879, Americans slept an average of 10 hours a night; today, they sleep an average of 6.9 hours a night on week nights and 7.5 hours a night on weekends.

16 It's a dog's life

You can **check in your dog or cat** for the night at the Pet Inn Royal, at Tokyo's Narita Airport, or for the hour at the Gang dos Bichos – the world's first love hotel for pets – in São Paulo. But if your pooch is in more need of a pamper, then the El Monte Sagrado Living Spa in the USA may be more up his street; the spa has its own "animal communicator" to help Fido unwind after a hard day chasing postmen.

17 From terrorism to tourism

If the underground dwellings in Spain and Turkey leave you cold, then perhaps the mountains of east Afghanistan will be more up your street: a former mujahaddin warlord is investing $10million in a new hotel complex overlooking the Tora Bora caves, where Al-Qaeda leader Osama Bin Laden hid out to avoid US forces in December 2001.

18 Weird things you could find in your hotel suite

- A single-lane bowling alley in the Penthouse Suite in the Hard Rock Hotel, Las Vegas.
- A three-metre-tall, champagne-flute-shaped hot tub in the Honeymoon Suite at Cove Haven, Pennsylvania.
- A recording studio in the Mooghotel, Sydney.
- A waterfall spa in the Renewal Suite at the Westin New York, New York City.
- A sleigh (with bells) in the Meguro Club Sekitei, Tokyo.

19 Things ain't what they used to be

▶▶ **Five types of buildings now commonly used as guesthouses**

- Riads (mansions set around a courtyard) in Morocco
- Estancias (sheep or cattle ranches) in Argentina
- Windmills in The Netherlands
- Castles in Scotland
- Rorbuer (fishermen's huts) in Norway

20 Getting away from it all

Hotel El Pangal gives new meaning to the word "remote"; stranded in the middle of the Pacific Ocean, on the aptly named Isla Robinson Crusoe, it is more than 600km from mainland Chile and can only be reached by a two-and-a-half-hour private charter from Santiago.

21 Meet and greet

▶▶ **Five ways you could be greeted at reception**

In France A kiss on both cheeks
In Zambia A gentle squeeze of the thumb
In Tuvalu A face pressed to the cheek, and a deep sniff
In Oman A handshake, followed by a kiss on the nose
In Mozambique Three hand claps and a "hello"

22 Checking out

Some hotels are known for the unfortunate fact that their celebrity guests expired while in residence.

Chateau Marmont, LA	John Belushi
Chelsea Hotel, New York	Sid Vicious and Nancy Spungen
D'Alsace pension, Paris	Oscar Wilde
Hard Rock Hotel, Las Vegas	John Entwistle
Hilton Hotel, Cardiff	Gene Pitney
Joshua Tree Inn, California	Gram Parsons
Landmark Hotel, LA	Janis Joplin and Divine
Ritz Carlton, Sydney	Michael Hutchence
Sheraton Hotel, Boston	Eugene O'Neill

23 **Places to Stay playlist**

- **Heartbreak Hotel**, Elvis Presley
- **Blue Hotel**, Chris Isaak
- **Chelsea Hotel #2**, Leonard Cohen
- **Hotel California**, The Eagles
- **Hotel Intro**, Moby

"Either the wallpaper goes, or I do."
Oscar Wilde on his deathbed in his Left Bank hotel, Paris

24 **The Library Hotel**

The ten floors of The Library Hotel in New York are arranged according to the **Dewey Decimal Classification** (DDC), a proprietary system of library classification developed by Melvil Dewey in 1876. The DDC organizes all knowledge into ten main classes – which are then subdivided into ten divisions, with each division having ten sections – using decimals as a means of categorization. Each of The Library Hotel's sixty rooms is filled with books that reflect its theme – there are more than six thousand books throughout the hotel.

▶▶ **A couple of floorplans of The Library Hotel**

Eighth floor: Literature
800.006 Mystery
800.005 Fairy tales
800.004 Dramatic literature
800.003 Poetry
800.002 Classic fiction
800.001 Erotic literature

Ninth floor: History
900.006 Biography
900.005 Geography and travel
900.004 Asian history
900.003 Oceanography
900.002 Ancient history
900.001 Twentieth-century history

25 Five great spas

Royal Malewane, South Africa Watch wildlife while you get a back rub in the Bush Spa.

Les Sources des Caudalie, France Michelin-star food for the calorie-conscious.

Ananda, India Try one of nearly eighty Ayurveda treatments in the foothills of the Himalayas.

Baan Thai Wellness Retreat, Thailand Peace and tranquillity at a royal household in the heart of Bangkok.

Gleneagles, Scotland Treat yourself to a massage after hacking round eighteen historic holes on the King's Course.

Ultimate
experiences
Places
to Stay
small print

ROUGH GUIDES – don't just travel

We hope you've been inspired by the experiences in this book. There are 24 other books in the 25 Ultimate Experiences series, each conceived to whet your appetite for travel and for everything the world has to offer. As well as covering the globe, the 25s series also includes books on **Journeys, World Food, Adventure Travel, Ethical Travel, Wildlife Adventures** and **Wonders of the World**.

When you start planning your trip, Rough Guides' new-look guides, maps and phrasebooks are the ultimate companions. For 25 years we've been refining what makes a good guidebook and we now include more colour photos and more information – on average 50% more pages – than any of our competitors. Just look for the sky-blue spines.

Rough Guides don't just travel – we also believe in getting the most out of life without a passport. Since the publication of the bestselling Rough Guides to **The Internet** and **World Music**, we've brought out a wide range of lively and authoritative guides on everything from **Climate Change** to **Hip-Hop**, from **MySpace** to **Film Noir** and from **The Brain** to **The Rolling Stones**.

Publishing information

Rough Guide 25 Ultimate experiences Places to Stay Published May 2007 by Rough Guides Ltd, 80 Strand, London WC2R 0RL
345 Hudson St, 4th Floor,
New York, NY 10014, USA
14 Local Shopping Centre, Panchsheel Park,
New Delhi 110017, India
Distributed by the Penguin Group
Penguin Books Ltd,
80 Strand, London WC2R 0RL
Penguin Group (USA)
375 Hudson Street, NY 10014, USA
Penguin Group (Australia)
250 Camberwell Road, Camberwell,
Victoria 3124, Australia
Penguin Books Canada Ltd,
10 Alcorn Avenue, Toronto, Ontario,
Canada M4V 1E4
Penguin Group (NZ)
67 Apollo Drive, Mairangi Bay, Auckland 1310,
New Zealand
Printed in China

80pp
A catalogue record for this book is available from the British Library
ISBN 13: 978-1-84353-833-2
The publishers and authors have done their best to ensure the accuracy and currency of all the information in **Rough Guide 25 Ultimate experiences Places to Stay**, however, they can accept no responsibility for any loss, injury, or inconvenience sustained by any traveller as a result of information or advice contained in the guide.
1   3   5   7   9   8   6   4   2

Rough Guide credits

Editors: Samantha Cook, Ruth Blackmore
Design & picture research: Scott Stickland, Chloe Faram, Monica Visca, Diana Jarvis, Jj Luck
Cartography: Katie Lloyd-Jones, Maxine Repath

Cover design: Diana Jarvis, Chloë Roberts
Production: Aimee Hampson, Katherine Owers
Proofreader: David Paul

The authors

Kate Berens (Experience 1), Editorial Director at Rough Guides, has travelled widely in South and Central America. Greg Ward (Experience 2) has written numerous Rough Guides, including the Rough Guide to the USA and Rough Guide to Southwest USA. Daisy Finer (Experiences 3, 18, 20 and 25) writes for Condé Nast Traveller among other publications. Jan Dodd (Experience 4) is the author of a number of Rough Guides, including the Rough Guide to Japan. Sarah Eno (Experience 5) caught the travel bug in her native California and is now a Travel Editor at Rough Guides. Keith Drew (Experiences 6, 8 and 11; Miscellany) is a Senior Editor at Rough Guides and a freelance travel journalist. Jonathan Buckley (Experience 7), the author of the Rough Guide to Venice, also co-authors the Rough Guide to Italy and the Rough Guide to Tuscany and Umbria. Alison Murchie (Experience 9) has travelled and worked in eastern Europe and is a Travel Editor at Rough Guides. Ross Velton (Experience 10) is the author of The Naked Truth About Cap d'Agde. Andrew Benson (Experience 12) wrote the Rough Guide to Argentina. Norm Longley (Experience 13) is the author of the Rough Guide to Slovenia. AnneLise Sorensen (Experience 14), who is half-Catalan, has lived in Spain and written about the country for numerous guidebooks, magazines, and websites. Marc Dubin (Experience 15) has written numerous Rough Guides and is co-author of the Rough Guide to Greece. Andrew Rosenberg (Experience 16), Executive Editor at the Rough Guides New York office,

has travelled extensively in Europe. **Richard Trillo** (Experience 17) has written numerous Rough Guides and is the author of the Rough Guide to Kenya. **Charles de Ledesma** (Experience 19) is the co-author of the Rough Guide to Malaysia, Singapore and Brunei.
Melissa Graham (Experience 21) is co-author of the Rough Guide to Chile. **Donald Reid** (Experience 22) is co-author of the Rough Guide to Scotland. **Mark Fass** (Experience 23), a Brooklyn-based writer, has written for The New York Times and New York Magazine, among others.
Mark Ellwood (Experience 24) is co-author of the Rough Guide to Florida.

Picture credits

Cover © Royalty-Free/Corbis
2 Courtesy of Termas de Puyuhuapi
6 Courtesy of Icehotel
8 Courtesy of Blancaneaux Lodge
9 Mayan carving ©Danita Delimont/Alamy; Mayan ruin ©Danita Delimont/Alamy
10 Courtesy of La Posada
11 La Posada interiors, courtesy of La Posada; Trains at Winslow, Arizona ©Greg Ward/Rough Guides
12–13 Courtesy of Oberoi Hotels
14–15 Courtesy of Hiiragiya ryokan
16–17 Courtesy of Casa Lalla
18–19 Courtesy of Chole Mjini
20 Courtesy of Hotel Danieli
22–23 Courtesy of Icehotel
25 Horse and cart ©Stephanie Prior
26 Beach games at Cap d'Agde ©Ross Velton; Shopping at Cap d'Agde ©Ross Velton
26–27 Beach at Cap d'Agde ©Cris Haigh/Alamy
27 Signpost at Cap d'Agde ©Cris Haigh/Alamy
28–29 Courtesy of Ongava Game Reserve
30–31 Horse trekking in Argentina ©Paul Springett/Alamy
32–33 Courtesy of Hostel Celica
34–35 Arcade in Palacio de Rajoy, Pazo de Raxoi, Praza do Obradoiro, Santiago ©Ian Dagnall/Alamy
35 Hostal de los Reyes Catolicos, Santiago de Compostela ©Jean Dominique Dallet/Alamy; Cathedral, Santiago de Compostela ©Matthew Jackson/Alamy

36–37 Courtesy of Mount Áthos Pilgrim's Bureau
38–39 Gellért baths ©Eddie Gerald/Rough Guides
40 Malewa River Lodge hut with balcony ©Richard Trillo; Out riding ©Richard Trillo
41 Huts ©Richard Trillo; River crossing ©Richard Trillo
42–43 Courtesy of Soneva Gili
44 Longboat ©Neil Emmerson/Robert Harding; Longhouse on stilts ©Neil Emmerson/Robert Harding; Relaxing on the veranda at a longhouse ©Derek Brown/Alamy
46 Exterior of the Burj Al Arab ©Alamy
47 Interior detail of Burj Al Arab ©Arco Images /Alamy; Burj Al Arab lobby ©Yadid Levy/Alamy; Luxury interior at Burj Al Arab ©Patrick Frilet/Hemis/Alamy
48–49 Courtesy of Termas de Puyuhuapi
50–51 Interior of Kinloch Castle ©Michael Jenner/Robert Harding Picture Library Ltd/Alamy
52–53 An abandoned yacht washed up on the beach at Tulum ©Scott Stickland
52–53 Courtesy Casa Magna
54–55 School of bannerfish ©Gorgette Douwma/ImageState/Alamy
54 Delivery arriving at Jules' Undersea Lodge, courtesy of Jules' Undersea Lodge
55 Watching TV at Jules' Undersea Lodge, courtesy of Jules' Undersea Lodge
56–57 Courtesy of Pousada Maravilha
58 Courtesy Casa Lalla

Fly Less – Stay Longer!

Rough Guides believes in the good that travel does, but we are deeply aware of the impact of fuel emissions on climate change. We recommend taking fewer trips and staying for longer. If you can avoid travelling by air, please use an alternative, especially for journeys of under 1000km/600 miles. And always offset your travel at **www.roughguides.com/climatechange**.

Over 70 reference books and hundreds of travel
guides, maps & phrasebooks that cover the world